Oxfordshire & Wiltshire

Edited By Sarah Olivo

First published in Great Britain in 2019 by:

Young Writers
Remus House
Coltsfoot Drive
Peterborough
PE2 9BF
Telephone: 01733 890066
Website: www.youngwriters.co.uk

FOREWORD

Here at Young Writers, we love to let imaginations run wild and creativity go crazy. Our aim is to encourage young people to get their creative juices flowing and put pen to paper. Each competition is tailored to the relevant age group, hopefully giving each pupil the inspiration and incentive to create their own piece of creative writing, whether it's a poem or a short story. By allowing them to see their own work in print, we know their confidence and love for the written word will grow.

For our latest competition Poetry Wonderland, we invited primary school pupils to create wild and wonderful poems on any topic they liked – the only limits were the limits of their imagination! Using poetry as their magic wand, these young poets have conjured up worlds, creatures and situations that will amaze and astound or scare and startle! Using a variety of poetic forms of their own choosing, they have allowed us to get a glimpse into their vivid imaginations. We hope you enjoy wandering through the wonders of this book as much as we have.

CONTENTS

Grace Lily Boswell (8)	68
Isabelle Kirtland (7)	69
Max Emmett Rowark (8)	70
Keeley Claridge (8)	71
Ethan Palczynski (7)	72
Roman Clark (9)	73
Jonathan Alan Paver (8)	74
Liam Rodrigues Pacheco (7)	75
Emily Jane Tack (8)	76
Ethan Shields (7)	77
Christian Filica (7)	78
Joshua Oakley (9)	79
Harry Deans (9)	80
Lois Dolder (8)	81
Mason Clark (7)	82
Jacob Titchner (7)	83
Jacob Robert Sarabia-Lock (8)	84
Leo Kavanagh (9)	85
Tianna Duffy (7)	86
Thomas Harper (8)	87
Ollie Clarke (9)	88
Sophia Troy (8)	89
Harry Clark (8)	90
Bradley John Denham (8)	91
George Maguire (8)	92

Calder House School, Colerne

Seth Couch (10)	93
Henry Coxall (8)	94
Oliver James Knockton (9)	95
Ashley Ellen Byers (9)	96
George Northway (9)	97
William Hodgson (8)	98
James Peeroo (9)	99
Archie Corbett (8)	100
Xavier Atkinson (10)	101
Max Weston (8)	102
Oliver John Mackenzie Rose (10)	103

Charter Primary School, Chippenham

Jessica Erin Tidmarsh (9)	104

Lily Woodhouse (10)	106
Poppy Alice Hurkett (10)	108
Troy Wells (9)	110
Aeryn Spearing (9)	112
Adam Rickards (9)	113
William South (9)	114
Soraya Milani Coombs (9)	115
Joshua Billing (9)	116
Jack Thomas Christopher Pottinger (9)	117
Miriani Wingert (9)	118
Natalie Stew (10)	119
Antonio Andrei Dobre (9)	120
Joshua Flynn (9)	121
Zach Dawson (9)	122
Alpha Jallow (9)	123
Jacob Connerty (9)	124

Frieth CEC School, Frieth

Ivy Nell Gillespie (10)	125
Ella Hayter (9)	126
Ella Nickolls (10)	128
Daniel Hawes (10)	130
Ruben Oldham (10)	132
Ellie Pash (9)	134
Eleanor Nancy Monks (9)	136
Henry Harbinson (10)	137
Joshua D Turner (10)	138
Xanthe-Rose Ann Bayliss (9)	139
Imogen Sharp (10)	140
Freya Roslyn Randall (9)	141
Mary (10)	142
Freddie Lee (9)	143
Cleo Coombs (8)	144
Leah Maxwell (9)	145
Jessica Lily Dale (8)	146
Tom Yoxall (10)	147
Evie Crowther-Birch (8)	148
Georgina Lee (10)	149
Emily Forder (8)	150
Annabelle Groom (10)	151
Oscar Deakin (10)	152
Alice Farrow (8)	153

Phoebe Coombs (10)   154
Enzo Xavier Chiappe (10)   155
Willow Anderson (9)   156
Charlotte Tedder (10)   157

King's Lodge Primary School, Chippenham

George Powlson (10)   158

Old Sarum Primary School, Old Sarum

Imogen Hibberd (9)   159
Lexie Taylor Redman (10)   160
Isobel Moody (9)   162
Harriet Josephine Langley (9)   164
Brooke Lewis (9)   166
James Tovey (9)   167
Orlagh-Mai Erin Tyrrell (9)   168
Elly-Mae Willock (9)   169
Lily-Ann Marie Keating (9)   170
Owen Otter (9)   171

THE POEMS

Candyfloss House

C hewy, delicious sweets
A mazingly perfect candyfloss
N icely made and fresh
D electably nice
Y ummiest I've ever tasted from the Ferris wheel
F antastically fantastic
L ots of people come to see
O utstanding rating from me
S o amazingly precious
S o perfectly perfect from the candyfloss stand

H ow amazing
O n a top-notch company
U tterly great from the bumper cars
S o delicious
E veryone comes to have a bite.

Orianne Molloholli (8)

1

Dragon Disco

A dragon disco, oh, what fun,
I have a plus-one, so why don't you come?
It's down a fox hole, but don't you worry,
It's worth it for the bubble flurry,
Oh, yummy, there's a barbecue,
With burgers and sausages, but mind you,
Their bacon rolls are tasty too,
Hooray! There is a disco floor!
With flashing lights and much, much more,
Uh oh! Fire! Mind your head,
That dragon woke up on the wrong side of his bed,
Oh, yay, limbo! How low can you go?
"Ow!" I bashed the bar on my second go,
I'm getting tired, time to go home!

Keiraleigh Baker (10)
Amesbury Archer Primary School, Amesbury

The Mythical Pig

The pig was found in a land with cows for clouds,
Chocolate trees with mint for grass,
And ice cream for a sky.
The pig can fly, the pig can fly!
How and why can he fly?

I lick the grass and trees,
All I taste is mint and chocolate.

The pig told his goal to the moon,
For food,
And asked, "Why do you live,
Five-hundred feet in the sky?
I'm leaving now,
Goodbye."

Jack Jackson (10)
Amesbury Archer Primary School, Amesbury

Monsters

M onsters are gloopy, monsters are green
O ver the years, they grew more mean
N ever will they become top of the class
S chool was hard but they will never pass
T he monsters quickly got on the bus
E ven though they were in such a fuss
R unning from the volcano in a rush, just to get
back to the wonderful school bus.

Ali Gutzwiller (10)

Amesbury Archer Primary School, Amesbury

Lunch With A Dragon

Today, I had lunch with a dragon,
It was weird, he brought food in a wagon.
It was time to eat a little treat,
With lots of cakes in different shapes,
I offered him tea, then he saw a bee,
I said, "Stand still!"
He said, "No, sir, it's time to leave,
Bye bye, little girl!"
And that was the end of the little tea party.

Jasmine Gibson (10)
Amesbury Archer Primary School, Amesbury

Sweet Monster

He walked through the park,
in the dark.
It was quite odd,
he brought a pod.
He sat on the grass,
eating the glass.
With a grunt
and a punch
he sat in a grump,
and said, "I'm bored, I'm bored, I ate all my food!
What a baboon!"
Eating sweets,
what a treat.

Jessica Parry (10)
Amesbury Archer Primary School, Amesbury

Chocolate Madness

My house made of chocolate is quite the delight,
Whenever I am hungry, I can just take a bite,
But when it is hot,
It melts quite a lot,
The roof, the walls, the chairs, the lot,
My mum, my dad, my siblings all moved out,
Sadly, now, I live all on my own,
Even I don't have a home.

Brooke Nash (11)
Amesbury Archer Primary School, Amesbury

Explosive Trouble

On a magical moon made of sweets,
It had holes for one reason,
For one sheep was explosive,
Explosive trouble everywhere,
You just can't sleep,
Because your house is a heap,
This will not keep you safe,
From this booming sheep!

Leo Mackman (10)
Amesbury Archer Primary School, Amesbury

The Unicorns

U nique things I saw in the expensive house

N ext door had it all, from weird, wild to unusual

I was just about to go to Candy Land when the noisy animals

C ame again and I was getting really annoyed with it!

O h, what annoying, cheeky things

R ustling trees outside because the things were fighting

N ever saw things like this before in my life

S o they had to be naughty unicorns!

I n midair, the unicorns went flying through the clouds

N ext, they played hide-and-seek

M y mouth was open with amazement

I t was so imaginative that I ran home

D ad said I couldn't have a unicorn of my own

A unicorn flew into my pink unicorn room

I had my eyes like goldfish because it was so elegant

R unning away, I called my dad because he was at work.

Freya Wilson (8)

Barley Hill Primary School, Thame

The Circus

The waft of sawdust crept up my nose,
mixed with the early smell of dew and rose,
as I saw a cup of tea and had a quick dose.
I strolled into the stripy tent,
and swung on my trapeze that was a bit bent,
as I put on my leotard, pushing out the dents,
I looked in my mirror and tied back my hair,
thinking to myself, *this is much better than the fair*
with tightrope walkers and majestic mares.

The performance is starting! Quick! Hurry up!
I had butterflies in my tummy as I sipped from a
cup,
I took a deep breath and stepped in the ring,
as the speaker played and started to sing.
I swung on my trapeze, flying in the air,
as the audience was thinking, *this was worth the*
fare!

That night, as I was curled up in bed,
my mum told me something, and I said,
"I love being in the circus!"

Yasmin Ghazi (8)

Barley Hill Primary School, Thame

Wow!

I went to the colossal moon, the colossal moon,
When I got there, I found a chick, a huge chick,
Just sitting there, drinking soda - really, soda!
She offered me a bit and I had a little sip,
But, to my surprise, it made me spit!
A bad taste in my mouth.
The chick had a sip, but did not have a little spit,
My jaws split when I saw its huge mum,
Who had a huge sip but did not spit.
"Wow!" I said, aloud,
She just didn't spit,
My jaws again split at the sight of the sip,
I tried another little sip, but I still had a little spit.
The chick wore a clip as she began to sip,
Sip, sip, sip, no spit, no spit,
I could hear *sip, sip*, no spit.
I could smell soda,
Again I tried a sip, but still had a spit,
Why did I go to the moon?
The chick begged for me to have another sip,
No spit!

May Bell (7)
Barley Hill Primary School, Thame

My Pet Dragon Spiky

My pet dragon Spiky
is rather very tiny.
He's an adorable baby
all clean and scaly.
He jumps in the garden moss
his favourite food is candyfloss.
With his cute little body
and cute little wings
he plays about with all sorts of things.

Although...

He picks his nose
and bites his toes.
He roly-polys everywhere
like he really doesn't care!
He reeks of fish
and eats my dish.
He runs in the house
and chases my pet mouse.

Ruined carpets
torn sofas
snapped tables
ripped bed covers
scratched tiles
peeling paint
scraped cupboards...

I took him to the local pet store
to see if they can do anything more.
Now I visit him every day
but he is all locked away...

Don't ever get a pet dragon under any
circumstances!

Imogen Keyte (8)
Barley Hill Primary School, Thame

The Fancy Frog

Once, there was a fancy frog
who lived in a giant bog
also, he was very bossy
because his bog was really mossy.
Deep underwater, down below
he liked to play his cello
but when it was winter and started to snow
oh boy, you wouldn't mess with this fellow!
He was grumpy and he was rude
yes, he loved to be in that mood.
His name was Phranks
and he loved playing warfare with his tanks.
I loved playing with that frog
he was the best tadpole there ever was
now he lives in my pond
I love him more than ever before!
When his bog went *kaboom!*
he came running into my room
he said hi, I said hello
he felt like a friendly fellow!

When he hopped into my bog
he felt like a friendly frog.
When he left, I was scared
but then he came back in the end.

Harvey Woods (8)

Barley Hill Primary School, Thame

Blue Flamingo

This thing with a beak
Liked to play hide-and-seek
He loved snow
But never put on a show

Once, he went on a plane
On holiday to Spain
He didn't like it there
So he went back to his lair

Although he was blue
He normally needed the loo
So tried to go on holiday again
Some said he was lame

This was better
But then he got a letter
It was very cool
However, no pool

Sat down for a Pepsi Max
Remembered about the axe

It had orange legs
And a bundle of eggs

He said, "Relax."
A snowman said, "Chillax."
He was the opposite of fluffy
And forgot his coat that was tufty

Time for a nap
Maybe on an app
Smell the chocolate fountain
From high on a mountain.

Maisie Brown (8)
Barley Hill Primary School, Thame

Unicorns Fluffy

U nique singing, bright, never feel the light

N ever fear, I'll be here to save your candyfloss

I ce-cold ice cream, you might get brain freeze

C roak of a red kite swooping down and picking up food

O range carrots for bunnies, nibble, nibble, nibble, my tummy rumbles!

R aw potatoes ready to eat, they melt in your mouth, yummy!

N o more fuss, I've got to get on the bus, green pus on the tree

F righteningly freezing, wear a warm jacket to keep you snuggly

L ike a lolly, silky smooth as a dolly, red, blue, purple

U gh, yuck, I do not like lemon, yellow and sticky

F luffy candy

F loss, silky and bumpy lumpy

Y ellow, sticky, cold in a jug, cloudy yellow lemonade.

Ruby Ellen Harris (7)
Barley Hill Primary School, Thame

The Underwater Fairy Garden Poem

F airies, fairies, small but magical

A fairy as cute as could be

I t's incredible, it's amazing, oh, yes please, do come!

R are, beautiful, bright blue dolphins splashing up and down

Y ou think it's fabulous - well, I did tell you to come see the surprise

G reat, more to see! Fun, playful fish and a wonderful seahorse

A round you, clicking red crabs, I haven't seen them in ages

R ound and round the rabbits bounce, trying to get the yummy food

D o you think there's more to explore? I especially like the tasty treats

E lephants honking, I love the diamonds and the singing mermaids and flowers

N o, no, I don't want to leave - oh well, see you next time!

Chloe Amaranayake (7)
Barley Hill Primary School, Thame

Food Galaxy

Once, I was in a food galaxy with foods of all kinds,
Burgers and sprinkles and doughnuts galore,
Peas as stars and an onion ring for the Milky Way,
everything made of food.
Smelling the sweet smell of foods everywhere,
Shooting stars as sprinkles and a burger as Saturn
with a ring of cheese.
I could taste the taste of plain, sweet air,
I could touch nothing.

Once, I was in a town made of food called
Foodville,
Everybody who lived there was made of pizza.
I went up, up, up and saw a palace,
Then I went down, down, down to go and meet
whoever lived there.
Then I realised it was the queen pizza,
So I ran and ran and ran!
Suddenly, I woke up in my bed,
Was it a dream or was it not?

Rosie Lewis (8)
Barley Hill Primary School, Thame

In The Sky

In the sky, I could see rainbows reaching across the
blue open space
looking a lot like a funny face
and pink fluffy birds
talking with very strange words
the snowy mountains high in the sky
it was as if I could fly!

As I looked around, I could see the sea
and monsters turning into cupcakes
but they looked very much like pancakes
I could hear the magical sound of unicorns
but it wasn't very loud

I could hear the roaring of rockets going by
and the sound of twinkling stars
I could even feel the heat of the blazing hot sun
it was as roasted as a bun
I could hear people chatting below
but not very loud

Then I came down from high in the sky.

Esther Stevenson (8)
Barley Hill Primary School, Thame

Watch Out, Chickens About!

One day when I walked out
I heard a shout
from a local water spout
It said, "The cheese shop is flying
and dropping meaty chickens!"

I dodged and darted all the plops
but they kicked me on the butt!
Soon, I saw a pile of sugar
and what a shock!
Out came blue and green liquorice.

And soon enough
I woke up in marshmallow
but still, a sherbet chicken said hello
by doing a plop.

I knew it was too much because
I nearly fainted
and I got painted
with the date

and I waited and waited
until I painted
I wonder why they fainted?

Rowan May (7)

Barley Hill Primary School, Thame

Alice In Wonderland

Inspired by 'Alice's Adventures in Wonderland' by Lewis Carroll

One day in May, there was a baby,
who took a piece of hay.
It landed in the sea,
and floated like crazy.
The baby smelt a cinnamon and gingerbread house,
suddenly, Alice found a cute and muscular mouse.
"Do you know where the white rabbit is?"
"Why, is that his?"
"Yes, it is his clock,
but it doesn't have a tick-tock."
"I have chocolate, would you like a piece?"
"Yes," said the mouse, Keith.
"It is so bright,
so why don't you stand out of the light?"
"Thank you for the chocolate,
I will have a good look."

Kiera Bousfield (9)

Barley Hill Primary School, Thame

Time Travel Sneezing

Sneezing, sneezing, a normal habit, but now it's getting more than that!
I've been to Mexico, India, Wales and Brazil!
Not nice when you have a bad case of the sniffles!

For years and years, I've embraced meanies spitting in my face!
I've been to China, Australia, Japan and even Canada!

I have had this for eight miserable years!
"Doctor, doctor, fix me please!
I am dreading whenever I'm going to sneeze!
An annoying habit to get
when you eat too much baguette."

"When I am older," I declare,
"everything will be fair."

Ellie Masterson (8)
Barley Hill Primary School, Thame

Lightning Party!

R iding lightning is so much fun
I t's absolutely unimaginable
D angerous it sounds, but it's not
E verything is fun up there

L ike everything, it's lovely and wonderful
I t's amazing and wonderful in the beautiful sky
G reat to be gliding through the air
H igh in the sky you fly gracefully like birds
T o be up there is spectacular
N o slowing down
I 'm relieved I didn't fall like a brick
N o time to waste and pick up the pace
G reat to feel the cold wind in your face.

Benjamin Gwatkin (7)

Barley Hill Primary School, Thame

Crazy Volcano

C *rack!* go the yummy biscuits
R acing up in the beautiful air
A mazing biscuits up in the nice, fresh air
Z igzaggy volcanoes keep teleporting away
Y ellow, disgusting biscuits now in the air

V ans come in a bigger colourful van
O h, how did the biscuits fall on my head?
L aughing at the special biscuits on my head
C *rack!* go bits of delicious biscuits
A nother one that is bright and colourful comes
N ow another wonderful one
O h, wow, the biscuits look magical!

Sam Georgiou-White (7)
Barley Hill Primary School, Thame

Drive A Submarine

D rive around with me, come on
R iding is the best
I n you come into my magical submarine
V ery colourful and crazy, see?
E mbarrassing, please don't try this at home

A nd crazy and weird

S ometimes cosy and sometimes not cosy
U nusual day of my life
B eing in the submarine is not a good idea
M ust not be sleeping in
A ctually tricky
R iding is so hard
I t's annoying
N othing can stop me
E xciting, but sometimes not.

Rosie Chamberlain (8)
Barley Hill Primary School, Thame

Sailing On A Sea Of Fire

I'm sailing on a water boat,
I don't know what to do,
I'm sailing on a sea of fire,
I can't believe it too!

Twisting and turning around the rocks,
I need to hold onto my socks!
I lick the boat, I don't know why,
But I find it tastes of pie!

The fire is roaring up above,
As I hear a sound which I just love!
The sound of wind rushing past,
And the sound of water against the mast.

Well, I suppose,
It's not that bad,
Sailing on a sea of fire,
When people think you're mad.

Max Gwatkin (9)
Barley Hill Primary School, Thame

I Rode A Dolphin On The Trampoline

I rode a dolphin,
splash, splash, splash!
The dolphin was epic,
it was stretchy.
The sea was blue,
and I could see it too.
The sea was wet,
and there were fish,
in the deep blue sea.
The waves were high,
and they were wet,
it was windy overhead.

I climbed on a trampoline,
and I bounced,
I crouched,
and it was fun.
I found it funny,
I found it relaxing.

I just couldn't stop,
but I really wasn't clear that I had to stop,
I ignored my brain,
carried on bouncing.

Tamsin Blight (7)

Barley Hill Primary School, Thame

Pancake Land

P ancakes on the ground with perfect toppings on top

A s you want to see a brilliant world of pancakes, you will want to eat a yummy topped pancake

N ice as a candy land, but with more toppings

C akes, pans will make some pancakes, raspberries, strawberries on top

A s yummy as some melted chocolate and strawberries, but better

K ilos of cake won't be enough, you will need a whole classroom-sized case to fit one pancake in

E xtra syrup, don't tell my mummy!

S yrup falling through the sky!

Evie Watford (8)

Barley Hill Primary School, Thame

The Underwater Fairy Garden

F airies are small but cute

A ny fairies are caring, but just not you

I saw lots of singing, spectacular mermaids in the crowd

R are, sparkling crystals floating around me

Y ummy, delicious food on the wooden tables

G ardens pretty with beautiful flowers

A round you, bright red crabs clicking their claws

R abbits hopping around the gardens

D elicious fruit growing from the small trees

E ggs boiled, hot and delicious

N ests hang from the bumpy trees.

Maddie Eacott (7)

Barley Hill Primary School, Thame

Flying Sweets

F unny flying sweets laugh
L ucky sweets win more sweets
Y ummy candyfloss
I ce-cold lollipops
N aughty lollipops
G ummy sweets

S our sweets
W onderful candyfloss
E normous lollipops
E lephants eat sweets
T offee sweets
S weets cracking

I was at the zoo
and I saw a lion that started to roar at me
so then I saw a sweet on the floor
which began to fly in the sky.

Abbie Rawlings (8)

Barley Hill Primary School, Thame

A Tiny Monster

A tiny monster was climbing a cliff
most normal people thought that was a myth
not this monster with spirit
as cake fell from the top, he would nibble it.

According to legend, on top there was treasure
nobody knew how much, because they couldn't
measure
guarding it was a dragon with many teeth
anybody trespassing, he would eat!

But the monster had a plan
he would tickle his fang
then wake him
then he would just about be done!

Lucas James Pearce (8)
Barley Hill Primary School, Thame

Be Friends With A Bumblebee

I was sat in my garden, waiting for the sun,
but I was in some pain because a bee stung my bum!

My mum said I needed a nappy,
which made me not very happy.

The bumblebee was so mad,
because I looked really sad.

We walked and talked for about a mile,
which made me want to smile.

I told the bumblebee, "I want to be a giraffe!"
Then me and Bumble had a laugh.

And now I have my friend,
to the very end.

Macie Danielle Randall (8)
Barley Hill Primary School, Thame

Ninja Fight

One day, I became a ninja
"Whatever can I do?"
Then all of a sudden, a ninja sausage
came from a corner
and we went to have a fight
and we both got a fire sausage sword
then the battle commenced that night!

Then I got a brain-storming idea
to be brave and use creativity
and spinning quickly, I was bestride him
and chopped him into little bits of sausage.
I won and I heard ninjas cheering
and I realised I was on Saturn!

Benjamin Parr (8)
Barley Hill Primary School, Thame

Thump, Crash, Bang!

Thump! Crash! Bang! as I fell
then someone rang a bell.
I was in Diagon Alley
it had a gallery.
I drank a potion
that went *kabang!*
Oh no! *Bang!*
It went quite wrong.
Oh no! It made a bog!
There were some hogs.

Thump! Crash! Bang!
The potions were very grand.
Cauldron sizzled, *bang!*
Oh no, someone got me with their wand
and I was in a pond!

Now I am back home...

Joseph Blest (8)
Barley Hill Primary School, Thame

Space Pugicorn

S oars everywhere
P lays in black holes and wormholes
A lways busy
C atches a ride in a wormhole
E ats delicious Mars bars

P ets his dragon
U ses a rideable cockroach
G ets on his cockroach
I gnites the lumpy space trash
C reates new sorts of boxes
O perates a rideable potato
R ides the rideable potato
N ow that's one of the 365 days of a year.

Ben Cleare (9)

Barley Hill Primary School, Thame

Little Dragons

L ittle dragons love to play
I like baby dragons that dance all day
T aming dragons till the next day
T iming my dragon till it gets grey
L ying down in the sun
E yelids flutter every day.

D ragons dancing in the bay
R oaring riot day by day
A running race on a Sunday
G o, go, go, let's run every day
O n holiday
N ow it's time to say g'day.

Isabel Mcmillan (7)

Barley Hill Primary School, Thame

The Crazy Village

I saw a crazy pigeon on a lake,
He flew away just on my face,
Oh no!
I brushed him with a brushing brush,
He flew away in a rush,
And ate a pizza with a gulp,
Wow!
I could smell a pizza on a kite,
So I ate it with a bite,
I saw a big brown box of gold treasure,
I tried to get it, but it flew away in the lake,
Instead of a man riding a horse, a horse rode a man,
A lion was drinking Coke,
A king had an old and dusty house.

Ansh Navinkumar Desai (7)
Barley Hill Primary School, Thame

Baking Tray World

Miniature scene
what a dream
a cottage on an upside-down teacup
a pet sugar pup
lolly trees
but no breeze
tiny little people
in the steeple
eat your biscuit
wouldn't risk it
living on a cupcake
what a mistake
the sugar dog wags its tail
but there's no hail
smelling a lemonade fountain
on the sugar mountain
cinnamon leaves
on the lolly trees
a world on a tray
just for display.

Lois Horsman (8)
Barley Hill Primary School, Thame

Lord Of Rings

L ord of Rings sat tight on his throne
O minous monsters were guarding his lair
R ings were everywhere in his lair
D anger, danger, the heroes were there!

O ff with a flash, they were in the lair
F ights were had and the bad guys came to a halt

R ings gone
I nto space
N ever seen again
G one, the bodies vanished
S afe, the universe was totally safe.

George Blight (8)

Barley Hill Primary School, Thame

Lavacorn

L ava down in this place, weirdos blow up in

A pig's face, till they land on a moon crater with a

V olcano and dancing dog killing aliens and cheese blocks.

A unicorn eating candy canes, yay! Cuddly cat, soft

C arrots, orange as oranges. Falling, calling in my head

"O h please, oh please, save me! A dragon and an angry

R hino are approaching. Will I live? Maybe.

N o, no, no! I lose...

Cody Bentley (7)
Barley Hill Primary School, Thame

Lemon Squash

I did not like swimming in lemon squash
it was so sticky and there were so many wasps.
The boiled sweets were scratchy
they made my feet sore
after one second, I could not take it anymore!
I wanted to get out of this pool right away
but I had to stay there all day.
Why did I make that stupid request?
Because swimming in there was not the best.
All the wasps that stung my face...
"I do not like this place!"

Chloe Gregory (7)
Barley Hill Primary School, Thame

Flying Car In The Air

Yesterday, I flew on a flying car
buying a shining car!
I went over and over a marshmallow
nearly like a hollow
it was there I saw a flying bus.
In the windy air, I flew
flying higher than a butterfly.
Not on bumpy roads
hearing the birds sing.
Rich or poor
makes no difference when you're in a flying car
everybody is the best.
I loved flying
but heard weird giggles
I heard more and more...

Dylan Pilgrim (7)
Barley Hill Primary School, Thame

Flying Tractor

Chug, chug, chug went the flying tractor.
The glistening flying tractor reversed,
The tractor connected to the plough,
It folded out its special wings,
The jet blasters turned on,
The tractor flew up into the air,
It started ploughing the clouds,
When it finished, it went back and started seeding,
That was done.
The flying sweet harvester flew up and harvested
the sweets.
People came to eat the sweets.

Joshua Foster (8)
Barley Hill Primary School, Thame

Invisible Crutches

Once, I went to a crutches stall
because I broke my leg
and all they said was, "Take a dare!"
So I said, "I'll take the invisible pair!"
I kept on falling.
"Hahaha!
You took the dare!
They're made of air!"
"How dare you, you're going to pay
me £30 every day,"
I would say.
"We'll pay you £15 a day."
"Okay."

Jake Handley (7)
Barley Hill Primary School, Thame

Alice In Wonderland

Inspired by 'Alice's Adventures in Wonderland' by Lewis Carroll

As Alice hopped to her house
She saw a cute mouse
"Do you know where the White Rabbit is?"
"Why, is that his?"
"Yes, it's his clock
It has got a tick-tock.
I have gummies, would you like one?"
Alice nodded. "Ah, the sun!"
"What's wrong? Is it too bright?"
"Yes." "Then stand out of the light.
Let's find the White Rabbit!"

Milly Stancombe (8)

Barley Hill Primary School, Thame

Pancake Land

I adore pancakes
drops of syrup on my tongue
pancakes for breakfast.

P our mixture in bowl
A s yummy as candyfloss
N utritious pancakes, mmm
C akes, all flavours, but not as good as pancakes
A mazing texture as soft as anything
K ept curled up like folded paper
E xtra syrup - shh, don't tell my mum
S yrup on my tongue - yum!

Olivia Aimee Muirhead (8)
Barley Hill Primary School, Thame

Candy Land

The chocolate dragon finally
drives the sticky chocolate spaceship
and falls on the candy dragon.

The sweetie dragon delivers
sticky chocolate... *boom!*
Everything covered in sticky chocolate!

There is a burger made
with onion rings around it.
There is a dragon made with sugar
Also a dragon made with slimy, sticky chocolate.
I like Candy Land!

Jack Parsons (7)
Barley Hill Primary School, Thame

Weird And Wonderful Creatures

The rattleclaw,
loves nothing more,
than to snuggle,
and snore,
on the kitchen floor.
When Mum comes in,
and calls, "Tom Flyn!"
it wakes up,
and gnaws on the door.

The chickenboar,
is worse, a lot more.
It squawks and squabbles,
screeches and caws.
When Mum and Dad,
come home for tea,
it's quiet - well, eventually!

Kayley Kidger (7)
Barley Hill Primary School, Thame

Hug Monster

As I was walking down the street
I saw some massive feet
he needed a hug
but then I would get a bug
he would feel so sad
then I would feel bad.

I was going to cuddle
I was a bit muddled
because I was happy
I wanted to change my nappy.

"Who wants to say goodbye
or hi?"
People could not be cold
when he had them in a hold.

Ewan Lewis (8)
Barley Hill Primary School, Thame

Rabbit In The Tree

When I was walking through the forest,
I saw a rabbit in the tree,
and I got it down,
safe and sound.
Then, when I got home,
I tried to see whose it was,
but it did not have a microchip,
so I kept it and it was so cute,
and it was a baby,
so that explained why it was cute!
A few weeks later, it caught a bad disease,
and died,
but I got over it.

Molly Ann Ward (7)
Barley Hill Primary School, Thame

Humpback Race

I raced a humpback whale,
It really was terrific,
But then I stopped to cut my charming, fab nails.
Suddenly, I looked up at the happy, huge
humpback whale.
I didn't know what the massive thing was doing.

He may have been disqualified,
Or did he need a long break?
Whatever he did need,
At least I won the big race!
Happy cheers for me, oh me!

James Amaranayake (7)
Barley Hill Primary School, Thame

Tiger Boy

T igers are friendly, what to do?

I play with them all day

G roups are what we play in, we love to play

E ven though when games start to get rough, we stop

R ough is never allowed

B ecause we play rounders, the games never end!

O h, also, we play some games for over a day!

Y ou are my friends, I love to play!

Daisy-Mae Moakes (9)

Barley Hill Primary School, Thame

Candy Land

There is a mouse who doesn't have a house.
You can hear the birds singing and see the white
clouds moving,
everybody having fun while the parents eat their
buns,
the kites swaying and people playing.
You can smell the lovely sweets and cakes and
candyfloss, more things,
but when the button rings,
it will all go away.
Everybody goes to this magical wonderland.

Chloe Pitts (8)

Barley Hill Primary School, Thame

The Shark

I loved my cool, amazing trip
on top of the magnificent blue ocean.
The tall man who was driving the shiny, gold boat
let us jump in.
Suddenly, something deadly grabbed my tiny leg
it was a shark,
a very hungry shark!
He thought my delicious leg
was a fish.
A few hours later,
me and bad-looking shark
made really good friends!

Herbie Spencer Kennneth Baker (7)
Barley Hill Primary School, Thame

Water Stingray

In the water, I went to see the mean, deadly stingray,
so I could take a picture.

In the water, it was really hard to move,
because it was like swimming.

If you touched the stingray, you'd get poisoned,
if the stingray touched you, you'd get really hurt.

I saw a boat and got on there,
on the boat, I was safe.

Oliver Sackett (7)
Barley Hill Primary School, Thame

Giant Chipmunk Wearing Chef Clothes

One day, a gigantic chipmunk rose,
With lots of hair and big fat toes
Also, he was wearing chef clothes,
But then he asked the butcher for some meat,
But all he got was a wisp of heat
Then he found a big fat pig,
So he thought he'd get it a wig,
He chased the pig round and round,
But all he got was a thumbs down.

Jacob Patrick Begley (7)
Barley Hill Primary School, Thame

An Underwater Explosion

One ordinary day
I was underwater
doing something not so ordinary.

With a laptop and laptop fish
it seemed like my laptop fish battery saver
had come alive!

My computer kept on turning on and off
the battery was charging from 0% to 100%
now I was getting really annoyed
and my computer exploded!

Oliver Tapping (8)

Barley Hill Primary School, Thame

The Donkey That Flew To The Moon

Once, there was a donkey,
he liked to be silly.
Once, he went for a walk,
he found a block of dynamite,
and TNT.
He ran back to his house,
and grabbed a helmet and a lighter.
He put the helmet on,
and lit up the block of TNT,
and flew into space like a flying chicken,
and landed on the moon.

Ben Beerling (7)
Barley Hill Primary School, Thame

Hear Books Talking

I went to the library,
It was weird even as I stared,
I didn't know why the books could fly,
One big red one said, "Hello!"
One pink small one bellowed, "Get out!"
I rented a book and went home,
And finally, I was all alone,
And I accidentally took the pink one home.
Oh no!

Cleo Ramsay (7)
Barley Hill Primary School, Thame

One Moon

O nce, I saw a moon with macaroni on
N o one had visited it before
E verybody was on Earth apart from me in space

M ummy was scared, but I was fine
O h my, a moon eating macaroni!
O h no, macaroni falling into craters!
N ow I'm back home, my dad is happy.

Benjamin Graham Davis (7)
Barley Hill Primary School, Thame

Fish Model

M agical and pretty fish
O h, how their colours blind me
D o they know they shine?
E ven they walk like stars
L iving underwater

F ish really like to disco
I like to disco too
S he likes to boogie, boogie
H e likes her, he likes her.

Romilly Orchard (8)
Barley Hill Primary School, Thame

Trolls And Goblins

Trolls and goblins
always thumping
green and slimy
blowing trumpets
eating goats
scaring people
eating people
always on a roll
fighting giants
killing giants
snatching babies
eating babies
always on a roll
mashing brains
licking brains
travelling underground.

Harry Parsons (8)
Barley Hill Primary School, Thame

My Pet Dragon

I have a tiny, young pet dragon,
he really likes to play.
If he gets frustrated,
he will fight straight away.
He is extremely dangerous,
even when he's kind.
At the amazing, colourful sunset,
he will sleep quietly.
So now I can rest from all this craziness,
but I need to go to bed.

Tom Halson (8)
Barley Hill Primary School, Thame

Puppy World

P uppies are so fluffy
U nicorns the same
P uppies are the best
P retty puppy Poppy
Y ummy puppy food

W onderful company
O ut for walks every day
R unning around in circles
L ove the smell of them
D oggies are so cute.

Grace Lily Boswell (8)
Barley Hill Primary School, Thame

Tennis Match

A dog plays tennis with a cat
The dog eats so much that he gets fat
They both begin to chase the ball
It isn't good tennis at all!

The mad chicken runs to fly
But he ends up in France
For a bigger cup of tea
Everyone feels very surprised
They really cannot believe their eyes!

Isabelle Kirtland (7)
Barley Hill Primary School, Thame

Teleporting Goal

Once, there was a freaky, scary goal
Robert the hairy, scary, funny guy went in it
and he had a scary ride
and then because a cheesy, nice, lovely, colossal
macaroni bowling ball
and then a slimy, hilarious, flying octopus
he was so funky and lazy
and smelt the stinky smell of the Atlantic Ocean.

Max Emmett Rowark (8)
Barley Hill Primary School, Thame

Unicorns Eating Pancakes!

U nicorns love fluffy rainbows

N othing can stop

I love pancakes

C orns are from lawns

O reos, loved by unicorns

R eggie in the clouds, jumping around

N othing can be true, but unicorns are real

S ome things can be believed.

Keeley Claridge (8)

Barley Hill Primary School, Thame

Candy Crush

As I walked in Chocolate Land
I could barely stand
because there was so much
everywhere for me to touch
so much chocolate rain
falling from the sky
drifting through the sky so high
and marshmallow clouds with chocolate sauce and
sprinkles floated fast and high in the sky.

Ethan Palczynski (7)
Barley Hill Primary School, Thame

Video Games

V iral videos
I ndividual YouTubers
D ied, got to restart
E pic endings
O verpowered players

G aming away
A wesome moves
M ind-blowing games
E xtra levels to unlock
S ad times and funny times.

Roman Clark (9)
Barley Hill Primary School, Thame

Dragons

D ragons flying in the air
R obot dragons love to play every day
A ngry dragons breathing fire red as the sun
G lowing blue eye staring
O range dragons having lots of fun
N aughty dragons eating food
S ome dragons like to sleep.

Jonathan Alan Paver (8)

Barley Hill Primary School, Thame

Chocolate Fun

Spaceships land
and people run to see the chocolate inside.
Lovely aliens come outside
with the delicious chocolate in their hands.
Some of the chocolate comes with bands
connected to a parachute.
People take some bands sometimes
and play around with a lovely run.

Liam Rodrigues Pacheco (7)

Barley Hill Primary School, Thame

Crazy Chicken

I flew up to space
not expecting to see a chicken drinking delicious
soda
and eating amazing ice cream
also pecking bums
not letting me share her food!
Farewell, chicken friend
time to tell people
about my adventure.
Adventure completed
hip hip hooray!

Emily Jane Tack (8)
Barley Hill Primary School, Thame

The Rocket In The Night Sky

There is a fast rocketship in the night sky,
Because I like to fly,
But I don't know why,
But I really like to go amazingly high.

There is a colourful bird in the sky,
Because it likes to go really high,
And I don't know why, but he likes to fly high.

Ethan Shields (7)
Barley Hill Primary School, Thame

Marshmallow Land

When I woke, I saw a big marshmallow
and I was thinking
if I climb up, I will sunbathe
so I climbed and I sunbathed
and I felt something fall
and I heard something quiet
it was so quiet...
I opened my eyes and saw what was inside
the marshmallow.

Christian Filica (7)
Barley Hill Primary School, Thame

The Land Of Hell

It's ruled by Hellman
Hellman is a terror, so
Steal his cool quadspear

All he eats is figs
His kingdom is called Nic
Hell he gives to you

He kills lava pigs
He has an awesome Magmobile
He hates everybody

Mwahahaha!

Joshua Oakley (9)
Barley Hill Primary School, Thame

The End Of Mars And Earth

I got sucked into Mars
and I saw the amazing Union Jack around it
I also forgot, Mars is a jam tart
so, of course, I ate it
I came crashing down to Earth
and I had a massive poo
after a while, a massive explosion came
to be fair, it was my fart...

Harry Deans (9)
Barley Hill Primary School, Thame

My Go-Kart

There once was a bed
The bed was dead
It became a go-kart instead

It used to sleep
Now it goes *beep, beep*
It was in my brother's room
Now it goes *vroom, vroom*

It used to dream
Now it's a mean machine!

Lois Dolder (8)
Barley Hill Primary School, Thame

Hi Harry

Hi Harry, I see you lost your glasses.
Hi Harry, I see you lost your fastest broomstick.
Hi Harry, I see you lost your slowest broomstick.
Hi Harry, I see you're a wizard.
Hi Harry, I see you have a wand.
Hi Harry, I see you've learnt a spell!

Mason Clark (7)
Barley Hill Primary School, Thame

Chocolate Land

Chocolate is fun
this world is full of different species.

Cold chocolate is freezing cold
it makes you really cold.

Chocolate is full of happiness
it makes you fall asleep
and dream of yourself
flying through the air.

Jacob Titchner (7)
Barley Hill Primary School, Thame

Island Adventure

We found dinosaurs in a dino fight,
with coconut pies,
you know, the kind you like.
With a dino bite,
a light,
and fresh eyes too,
I winked at candy,
I winked at chocolate,
I winked at everything with my eyes.

Jacob Robert Sarabia-Lock (8)
Barley Hill Primary School, Thame

Flying Poop Chicken

I once had a chicken
who had a little kickin'
and when he got a rocket that he powered with
poop
he got inside and got to the moon
where he found an oily spoon.
When he got back to Earth,
he went back to his turf.

Leo Kavanagh (9)

Barley Hill Primary School, Thame

An Elephant Underwater

I saw an elephant underwater
I was looking for my daughter
Then my mum forgot my water
Then I went to get my water
When I went, I got some breath
Then my mother was such a bummer
I'd had enough for one day.

Tianna Duffy (7)
Barley Hill Primary School, Thame

I Lay On My Bed

I lay on my bed
with dreams in my head
I opened my eyes
and what a surprise
my Danger Mouse toy
was alive as a boy
reading Asterix and Obelix
and he read it for me.

Thomas Harper (8)
Barley Hill Primary School, Thame

Sports

S wimming, *splash, splash*
P addling in a boat
O lympics are the best
R unning past the others
T ake the lead
S ports are great.

Ollie Clarke (9)
Barley Hill Primary School, Thame

The Tiger

The tiger was sat on a log
ready to pounce on a frog
then, in the bog
the tiger thought he saw a dog
but through the fog
it turned out to be a hog.

Sophia Troy (8)

Barley Hill Primary School, Thame

Future

F uture is amazing
U nicorns are flying
T echnology
U nicorns are real
R ajasaurus, a new dinosaur
E xcellent!

Harry Clark (8)

Barley Hill Primary School, Thame

Underwater BBQ

I see bright yellow fish,
I feel so wet and damp
I can see mermaids swimming,
and they first eat all of the burgers.

Bradley John Denham (8)

Barley Hill Primary School, Thame

Autumn

A haiku poem

The leaves are falling
The birds are tweeting their songs
Now autumn is here.

George Maguire (8)

Barley Hill Primary School, Thame

In Duff Beer Land

In Duff Beer Land,
The Duff is as black as midnight,
All the food is flavoured with Duff,
Even the sweets are!

The Duff machine is as big as Everest,
You can eat anything, but you can't eat the houses!
Everything is black because Duff is black.
Even the sun is black!

They have to use edible black light,
Even the cars run on Duff,
Duff is the best!

Seth Couch (10)

Calder House School, Colerne

Ketchup Dragon

I was winning
So I started singing
And the ketchup dragon started grinning
And his name was Dilling
I was worried
He might go killing
So I started limping
In fear
And I did not cheer
Hold on, dear
Why here?
Such a majestic creature, its soft fur
And hard horns cutting the lawn
And how was he born?
Oh, some ketchup!
Ow! Hi, ketchup dragon!

Henry Coxall (8)
Calder House School, Colerne

Gummy Bear Land

In Gummy Bear Land everyone has a gun.
But don't worry, it's lots of fun!
The guns, they are not meant to kill.
They are only meant to give a thrill.
They don't shoot bullets,
They shoot bears that are gummy!
Open your mouth! They are very yummy!
But you must only think thoughts that are sweet!
Or the gun won't fire a single treat.

Oliver James Knockton (9)

Calder House School, Colerne

The Ten-Legged Turtle

Gliding high in the sea with my flippers
then going to see
if I dig low
there may be some food and tea.
I am slimy and I like to glide
so high that people can see me.
I am so slimy that the sand sticks on my body
so people can't see me.
I am so extraordinary
because I have ten legs.
It helps me swim with speed
then I can feed.

Ashley Ellen Byers (9)
Calder House School, Colerne

Candy Land

In Candy Land
the people cry candy
the houses are made out of lollipops
the world is made of chocolate
the world has billions of restaurants and sweet
shops
the trees are made out of jelly
the people are made out of candy
the glass is made out of jelly
the law says you can have nothing but sweets, just
sweets!

George Northway (9)
Calder House School, Colerne

The World Made Out Of Money

People think all money is gold
But it's cold and old
And foldable, stretchy and flexible
Money is smooth, flat and can be metal
I could buy a massive mansion
Or a car with a rocket engine
But money can't buy friends or family
You're better off thinking of being happy.

William Hodgson (8)

Calder House School, Colerne

In Candyland

In Candyland
The candy was as hard as a rock
And the candyfloss was as soft as a kitten
The slime was as sticky as a monster
And the trees were as hard as lollipops
And as sweet as a rocket
The shark was as fast as a jet plane
The ground was as soft as marshmallows.

James Peeroo (9)
Calder House School, Colerne

Ghosts And Toast

I am searching in the sea
To see which ghosts I can see
I see the water change, red, purple, green and blue
And the ghosts are like glue
The ghosts like putting up posts with other ghosts
And they like to boast
When we are making toast
We are met by Uncle Ghost!

Archie Corbett (8)
Calder House School, Colerne

In Wonderland

In Wonderland
a dragon like a jet
was sitting like a pet
in the wet.
Living in a reef of roast beef
drinking from an ice cream stream.
He could shrink
like a soft drink
with a wink.
He could run
like the sun
in a shotgun.

Xavier Atkinson (10)
Calder House School, Colerne

Underwater Football Pitch

I hear water crashing on the goal posts
I see fish swimming and I feel mud in-between my
toes
My socks are very wet
People are slipping on the wet mud and hurting
and not healing
People are scoring but falling and drooling and
drawing.

Max Weston (8)
Calder House School, Colerne

Pizzaland

In Pizzaland
the pizzas are fluffy
and the whole land is made of dough
and when you walk on the land
you will sink in
and when you launch a bomb
pizza goes everywhere!

Oliver John Mackenzie Rose (10)
Calder House School, Colerne

What A Crazy Town

This town is so noisy I can't hear myself think
these kids are prodding me in the back
it's frustrating!
What a crazy town this is!
The air smells like baked croissants,
and I can see dragons flying around my house!
There are thirteen-year-old gymnasts front-flipping
off the houses,
what a crazy town I'm in!
I'm on my way to the chocolate bear cave,
I've heard they are annoyed when they get woken
up.
Now I'm in the cave,
the brown chocolate bears are sleeping,
shh...!
Squash!
Oh no! I've stepped on some noisy goo,
now the bears have woken up!
Run!

I think I'm safe now,
but I'm on this strange island.
I can see men stroking a wild leopard.
"Excuse me, where am I?" I say curiously.
"You're on Strange Island," says one man.
I look at him and apologise for disturbing them,
and go off the island.
I go back to Crazy Town,
everything is quiet,
apart from the dragon's snoring,
and people are asleep all over the place.

What a crazy town!

Jessica Erin Tidmarsh (9)

Charter Primary School, Chippenham

My Adventure In My Land

I fell asleep at night
and fell into a land of unicorns and rainbows
and other things of delight.
I went to have a wander
to see what was around
and found a weird creature
that was wandering around.
I went to see what it was
it was something very odd
a creature of mixed up animals
eating lots of buns.
It was eating very fast
it was eating very quick
then it ran away
super-duper quick!
So I had a look around
and found a load of quiet reading
and found a planet mouse
wearing hot dog glasses.
I found it very funny
I found it very smart

they looked so realistic
I thought they were real
so I went to get a hot dog
because they made me so hungry!
When I came back
the planet mouse was gone
I felt so sad that
I thought of singing a song
then I went to go home
and there I saw the two animals that I saw before!
We had a little party
we had a little dance
then I went home
and told my parents about my land.

Lily Woodhouse (10)

Charter Primary School, Chippenham

Kawaii Island

When I woke up in the morning, I could not believe
my eyes
It was much better than the beautiful sunrise
When I looked down, fluffy candy was on the floor
I saw a pink fluffy unicorn roar!
I named him Sugar and now he was mine.
The lunar eclipse was simply divine!
The thesramaid (a rainbow aqua horse)
Swam right round the coral course
The candy cane forest was awfully dark
Even when the purple foxes were making their
mark.
Flying saucers were buzzing around
With pink gummy bears singing
Which was a lovely sound.
The rainbow bunnies in the cove were happy
Dragons were eating trees that were sweet and
sappy
After all the excitement I had, I hoped Sugar would
not be bad

Then Sugar and I went back home to settle in my
bed
Shh!
Sugar is a sleepyhead.

Poppy Alice Hurkett (10)

Charter Primary School, Chippenham

Magical Lands

I walked on a red carpet,
and found,
Halloween Land!
I was so excited, even when someone told me,
"A house with chicken legs haunts here!"
I didn't believe them, but I went with it,
after forty-four hours of hilarious, frantic fun.

I walked through a door and found,
a mountain range!
I was overjoyed to find it,
although someone said there was a snow monster!
I was having so much fun,
I forgot about the snow monster!

I walked through a cloud,
and found,
Football Land!
I was even more excited about the football!
It sounded amazing!
I went straight away.

It was amazing!
I would highly recommend all of these!

Troy Wells (9)
Charter Primary School, Chippenham

Poetry Adventures

P oetry adventures are amazing!

O MG, you should know

E very poem is different

T he book of a thousand poems is an example

R eally

Y es, good poems need description

A nybody

D efinitely can write a poem

V egetarian burger as the moon, that's a poem idea

E verybody needs to know that they can write a poem

N ever suspect that you can't write one

T o write a poem, you have to go on a magical journey

U nbelievable, you can do anything when you write

R eally!

E lves invited to tea, learning to

S peak alien and cheesy moon rocks are my ideas!

Aeryn Spearing (9)

Charter Primary School, Chippenham

Crazy Places

Interesting place, but where am I?
Mountainous trees everywhere,
oh? Is that a T-rex?
"Amazing looks," I hear one sad man say,
I run away!
Gorgeous deer lick my face,
one follows me at a steady pace.
I fall over, what on earth?
A talking mushroom!
Never would I believe,
I'd meet a singing banshee!
Aww, what a cute baby dragon,
I'll call you 'Bob'.
The lake is rather chilly,
argh, a kraken!
Isolated caves,
no, actually, that's a giant bat!
Occasionally, Bob flies away,
but otherwise, it's a smooth day.
Now I'm happy,
and that deer is still following me at a steady pace.

Adam Rickards (9)
Charter Primary School, Chippenham

Candy Land

As I took a chunk out of the dragon
the bell began to ring
and candy ran all over Candy Land for an hour.
The hot tub was full of melted chocolate
and mega marshmallows.
When I pulled a lever
nothing happened!
But then a shudder, a shake
three ice skating dragons came along
and swept me off my feet and flew me to the land
of popping candy.
Then a shudder, a shake
a flood of rainbow candy swept me off the ground
and sent me to the hot tub filled with hot
chocolate.

William South (9)
Charter Primary School, Chippenham

Slime Lover

S lime is the best thing ever to me
L oving slime is my hobby
I bring it to the dinner table and
M um tells me off
E very time after dinner, I go up to my room and shout

"L ove you, night!"
O bviously, I lie to play with my slime, because if I don't, I'll
V iciously die
E ven though I probably won't, there's only one thing you should know
R ainbow slime is my favourite!

Soraya Milani Coombs (9)
Charter Primary School, Chippenham

Candy Football Land

F ootball is good
I s there anything else?
F IFA 19 is the best FIFA game
A quick one-two

A h, Gareth Bale
N BA is for basketball
D ennis Bergkamp

C amping for a day
A m I the king?
N ot the best
D on't be ashamed
Y ou won't cry anymore

L and of football
A m I the king?
N ot Dennis Bergkamp
D o you play?

Joshua Billing (9)
Charter Primary School, Chippenham

Weird Life

I saw a weird sparkle in the air
and guess what? It was a scorpion!
Flying cake pooping...
What a weird adventure!

Then I saw a monster going into a volcano full of
sick...
Gross!
What a weird adventure!

After that, I saw a moving burger
running and squirting chickens.
What a weird adventure!

But anyway... where am I?

Jack Thomas Christopher Pottinger (9)
Charter Primary School, Chippenham

Dojo Land

D ojos are the most adorable monsters ever!
O ften growing yummy lollies
J olly little creatures they are!
O therwise, they live quite far!

L ollies galore in their worlds
A llies of the mould!
N ever give them chocolate because it upsets them quite a lot!
D onkeys graze on the ocelots!

Miriani Wingert (9)
Charter Primary School, Chippenham

Unicorns Are Real But Be Yourself

U nicorns are real,

N ever treat people differently,

I n every country, unicorns rule the Earth,

C ome on everybody, unicorns are your friends,

O n top of the world, I am,

R ise up and be yourself! I'm a unicorn,

N ever be someone you're not,

S ee my horn glow as it shines on you.

Natalie Stew (10)

Charter Primary School, Chippenham

Basketball King

I could taste so many flavours
I could see so many colours
It was like a dream, there was a basketball pitch
I took a shot, it landed in
And five elves went screaming
"Woah!"
One thousand sweets rained down
I felt like a king
I met a basketball superstar
There was a tree with jelly instead of leaves.

Antonio Andrei Dobre (9)

Charter Primary School, Chippenham

Volcano Surfer

I see an erupting volcano
But first, I need a lightning bolt
Shall I ask Zeus?
Or shall I ask a lightning moose?
I get my lightning bolt
The ride down isn't what I expected
Instead, I go down and die
I should've changed my mind
Now, I want to fly.

Joshua Flynn (9)
Charter Primary School, Chippenham

Dream

D azzling golden slime trees

R easonably tall mountains where you find rare slime

E dinburgh's fresh ginger moose milk

A tap-dancing unicorn roaming the land

M eet all of them and come to my land!

Zach Dawson (9)

Charter Primary School, Chippenham

Candy Land

I live in a candy land with magical dragons and
deer
there is a sticky, slippery football pitch
that bounces you all around
candy cane forest, magical food and creatures
also, ice cream cone Everest
an amazing place to stay.

Alpha Jallow (9)
Charter Primary School, Chippenham

Fantasy

F amily of mountains
A mazing food
N ation with fun for everyone
T errific food
A big Statue of Liberty
S mall China town
Y ummy food for everyone.

Jacob Connerty (9)

Charter Primary School, Chippenham

Underwater Candy Land

As I dive down under, a new world meets my eye,
And a colourful fish passes by.
Suddenly, something is caught in my sight,
A sweet, sour ball to light up the night!

As a sly treat slips into my mouth,
The sweet sensation fills the whole south.
Gracefully, the surface is filled with chocolate boats,
I wonder how so many can stay afloat?

Softly, my feet touch the soothing sand,
Just as I discover a jelly bean band.
A stick of candy cane stands upright and proud,
As a bunch of Haribos gather round as a crowd!

As I look at this wonderful world one last time,
A mystical Haribo has a flavour of lime.
At last, I float up to the sky,
Calling my final word, "Goodbye!"

Ivy Nell Gillespie (10)
Frieth CEC School, Frieth

It's A Cookietastic Life

Hello, my name is Picklewiddletiddle, Pickle for
short, and here's a poem
That I wrote about my best day ever
Well, really, best life (kind of)!

"C ool!" I said, suddenly floating up to the clouds,

O ften, I would camouflage and float back down
to London!

O f course, I spent most of my time moonwalking,
though,

"K ing, King!" I yelled. "It's rainbow raining, it's
infecting London!"

"I t's... it's amazing! It hasn't rainbow rained in
ages!" said the king.

E ventually, it stopped. I was sad, so I carried on
moonwalking,

T o my surprise, it started rainbow raining again!

A nd it stopped again.

S o I looked down and my mouth dropped open,

T o my surprise, the rain, well...

I t had dyed the houses different colours,

C autiously, I stepped back,

L ifted my chair up and threw it on a house down below,

I t was metal like our houses!

F irst, I sat on my bed and then I went to

E at a marshmallow to calm down!

Ella Hayter (9)

Frieth CEC School, Frieth

Sorry Dobby

In a plane, we go up to the sky,
Then Lucius says, "Dobby, say 'bye bye'!"
He pushes me out and I fall, like, forever,
When I hit the ground, my head hurts more than
ever.

How could he do such a harmful thing?
Now all I can hear is a bong and a bing,
I walk on and on, not knowing where I am,
And there it is, a crash and a bam!

I come to a store,
Which seems to be a bore,
When a bird-like horse walks in,
And says, "I need to find the burger bin."

He says, "I lost my keys in the trash."
And then walks into the wall with a *bash!*
Then the manager says to me,
"Welcome to McDonald's, what will it be?"

I stand as stiff as can be,
He says, "Look, do you want a Happy Meal? You
can have it for free."

"Y-y-yes," I stuttered, stunned,
And then I got knocked on the head and it was all
blurred...

Ella Nickolls (10)

Frieth CEC School, Frieth

The Crazy Cookie Land

Once, I fell down a rabbit hole,
Then there was a fireman's pole,
Next, I saw a cookie land,
And there was a shark who needed a hand,
I was missing my mum a lot,
But then I found an abandoned plot,
I went to eat the floor, I had a munch,
But I forgot I'd just had lunch!
There was a shark next to the house,
So I chucked out the mouse.
I tamed the shark and I sang,
"How old are you? Old or young?"
We went to the cookie shop,
I was wondering about the plot,
But then I saw some monsters,
Half of them were loggers.
They started eating the house,
Then I gave them a cookie mouse.
I gave them a hug,
But one fell on a plug!
We had to eat her,

Her cat gave a purr.
I flew back to my house,
Then I ate a cookie mouse.
I asked my mum, "What's the time?"
She said, "You can't rhyme!"

Daniel Hawes (10)
Frieth CEC School, Frieth

If There Was A Dream Wonderland

I fall into a wonderland of dreams that can come true,
I look up and I see what looks like a McDonald's.
On a perfectly round candy cloud, the McDonald's drops, my favourite meal,
I try to catch a Big Mac as it falls to the ground,
Some shakes and some fries I try and catch too,
But my wish does not come true.
As I reach out to catch my meal,
A strange, nasty thing happens...
A flying pig in golden armour swoops down,
And steals my glorious grub!
I chase it round and round again until I gave up,
I think that, maybe the next time I try, I will have a bit more luck.

From that day on to this one,
I'm still not sure if it was a dream or not,
Maybe if it was a dream,
The next time, if I have it,

I will receive some luck,
And have a loveable meal for my stomach!

Ruben Oldham (10)

Frieth CEC School, Frieth

I Married A Prince

Let me tell you about my wedding day,
Where everyone goes, 'hooray'!
I'm marrying Prince William,
So now I'm in line and the queen of a million!
I smell the flowers all around,
And as I come down, no one makes a sound.
I feel the soft, smooth silk dress,
I calm down and use my hopefulness,
Hopeful that everything will go well,
And now I can tell,
That people will want to see me,
I hear people trying to see,
Bustling and shouting,
Now it is time to go on our outing,
We visit everyone in the town,
And I put on my crown.
Everyone goes wild,
But now, I wonder if I'm being a bit mild!
Okay, so everyone's gone absolutely crazy,
So crazy that the flowers droop (upsy-daisy)!

I love my life as Queen,
And now you know what I mean.

Ellie Pash (9)
Frieth CEC School, Frieth

Shopkin Candy School

S hopkins school is so much fun

H aribos make us run

O n hot days, lemonade cools us down

P oppy corn is really loud

K inder eggs are my favourite

I n my sleep, I chew on gummy bears

N ina Noodles, the head teacher

C ookie, Kooky Cookie, sweet and sugary

A Shopkins playtime is the best

N o time for a rest

D o not work too hard

Y ou will love gummy bears

S weets are what you eat

C heeky cherries and cheeky chocolate, so cheeky!

H olidays, you can stay

O n a super candy day!

O h, a spectacular experience

L olli Poppins will give you.

Eleanor Nancy Monks (9)

Frieth CEC School, Frieth

Pete's Adventure

Once, there was a dragon named Pete,
But the only thing was, he had such small feet,
He was red and black,
And had different sized spikes running all down his back.

He went to his friend Mike's,
And he said, "If you want a cure, it takes many hikes."
Pete set off to find the sweetie mountain,
And next to that, there was a chocolate fountain.
On the other side, he found the cure,
A well full of water, deep and pure.

Pete pulled it up,
And poured it into a cup,
He swigged it down,
And then looked at the ground,
He didn't make one single sound,
Pete shouted, "Hooray! I have normal feet!"
And he jumped up and down.

Henry Harbinson (10)
Frieth CEC School, Frieth

Planet Burger

I was flying to Planet Burger,
In my mushroom rocket with all-you-can-eat
mushroom buffet,
But I didn't like mushrooms!
As I started to step on the squishy, greasy meat
section of Burger Planet,
I heard a strange type of sound,
Then *splat!* Ketchup all in my face,
Then mayo too,
So I licked it off and started to watch,
Ketchup people having a war against mayo people,
So we quickly got back on the mushroom ship,
But I kept a baby ketchup and a bag full of greasy,
delicious burgers,
Goodbye, Planet Burger!

PS: Don't go to Planet Burger,
Because you might get ketchup in your face!

Joshua D Turner (10)
Frieth CEC School, Frieth

A Weird Day

T he garden fresh as a daisy

H andstanding in the middle of it

A s I was handstanding, I saw some pepperoni

T hen some crust, then a large slice landed on my head

S uddenly, I ran in and told Mum, but she did not believe me! I said...

"W hen I was handstanding, I felt crust!"

E ven though Mum didn't believe me, she stepped outside.

"I 'm sure," I said.

"R eally?" said Mum.

"D efinitely saw it." Then whispered under my breath, "I don't think she gets it. It's April Fool's Day!"

Xanthe-Rose Ann Bayliss (9)

Frieth CEC School, Frieth

The Squishy Mountain

As I climb to the top,
my foot goes *plop!*
I fall down the hill,
which gives me such a thrill,
then I get up again, when...
I find a pen that smells of cotton candy.
I colour the mountain in candy,
and find out that one pen can be very handy.
Now the mountain is squishy,
but what is wrong is such a pity:
it has no flake or sprinkles,
and they make my tongue tingle.
I see in the distance the delivery man,
who has the other things in his van.
As he puts them on,
my sadness has completely gone.
This is the end,
of the squishy trend.

Imogen Sharp (10)
Frieth CEC School, Frieth

Wonderland

W ow, what a sight to see!

O h, do you not know what I'm talking about? Wonderland, unique place, it is

'N ice' is what people say, I saw 'amazing'

D ragons are they, fire they burst

E ager to go there, what a sight to see

R ocky roads, sweets, fun, everything that you could even imagine

L ollipops, animals, and we can't forget the Queen of Hearts

A lso, her daughter Lissie Harts

N ice she is, but our time is almost over - sad, it is

D o not forget Wonderland ever!

Freya Roslyn Randall (9)

Frieth CEC School, Frieth

The Day I Went Mad

If I can remember correctly,
It was one dark night in February,
I felt it all with a start,
It was a sharp, sudden pain in my heart,
I felt the need to run free,
Flooding all over me.

The doctors, they said I was mad,
But I wouldn't have believed him if he was my dad,
On and on the argument went,
In and out the doctor was sent,
Not even one minute I got to myself,
Not even one minute to look at the bookshelf.

All of a sudden, I saw all the bees,
All of the flowers,
And all of the trees.

Mary (10)
Frieth CEC School, Frieth

If Jupiter Was A Meatball

Jupiter, Mars, Venus, Saturn, Uranus, Earth,
Mercury, Neptune and Pluto,
all turned into food!
Ice creams on Earth,
Mars had pizza,
and Jupiter was a meatball.
All the wonderful things were happening,
as the chocolate bird had a sing.
All the cookies from Mercury started to whoosh by,
"I wish it was always like this," I said.
As I lay in my candy bed,
in the morning, I saw a black hole,
dripping with syrup.
Then I woke up from my dream,
but I still wished Jupiter was a meatball.

Freddie Lee (9)
Frieth CEC School, Frieth

Best Birthday Ever

Oh, please Mummy,
for my birthday, can I have a pink bike,
or a bunny?
Or can you take me for a hike?

What's this?
A present for me!
I will open it,
let's have a see.

Come on, my friends,
let's open it,
let's see what's inside,
I hope it's a slime kit.

It whisks us to a magical world,
in the world are chihuahuacorns,
and candy that tastes like jam swirls,
and candy horns.

We have a lovely time,
in the world of rhyme!

Cleo Coombs (8)
Frieth CEC School, Frieth

144

Chocolate Catastrophe

I was running on the edge of Bon Bon Cliff,
Until my legs began to feel very stiff,
I tripped and started to fall down, down, down,
Oh no, oh no! I was going to drown!
Suddenly, *squelch!* I fell into the bog,
I started to feel a bit like a frog,
But no, no, no, I had to escape,
After all, I didn't want this to be my fate!
Lethal and dangerous, the chocolate bog was,
My temper rose and I began to feel cross!
Why did this catastrophe have to come?
After all, I was just having fun!

Leah Maxwell (9)
Frieth CEC School, Frieth

The Cloud World

I ate some cloud
Then I felt quite proud
As it tasted like candyfloss
I thought, as I gave my hair a toss

To my great surprise
On my side
Was a young girl
Whose hair looked like it liked to curl

When I was having so much fun
Someone said, "Come try this sun!"
This sun? This sun? What did he mean?
So I looked over and I couldn't believe what I'd just seen!

A yummy, yummy Mars bar sun
Which looked like loads of fun
Yum, yum, yum!

Jessica Lily Dale (8)
Frieth CEC School, Frieth

Time Travel

Hi, my name is Ever,
My dad is very clever,
He once built me a tool,
We named it after a jewel,
It was a time travel device,
Once, I accidentally got stuck in the age of ice,
The Ancient Egyptians were a friendly bunch,
They let me join them for some lunch,
In Rome, I watched them fight,
Gladiators with all their might,
WW2 had lots of violence,
Whereas modern days classes have a bit more
silence,
But now, let's go back to modern day,
Where all I want to do is play!

Tom Yoxall (10)
Frieth CEC School, Frieth

Dragon Island

A crispy fire burning in the corner,
baby dragons never getting older.
"I want more food!" came a little squeak.
"No, darling, you need sleep,
now rest your sleepy head,
and go to bed."
"No, no, no! I want some heff!"
"Heff? What's heff?"
"Heff is sleepy slime with chocolate chips."
"Oh no, no, no!"
"Oh yes, yes, yes!"
"Please just rest your sleepy head,
and have a delightful dream."

Evie Crowther-Birch (8)
Frieth CEC School, Frieth

If Saturn Was A Cookie

Gingerbread houses
With dark chocolate mice
And marshmallows shouting hellos
But I think they would rather go
To the white chocolate snow!
The forests here fill up tummies
With lots of yummies!
The marshmallows sing, about everything
And you will need a knee, to get to every tree
They grow candy canes, they heal all pains!
The rings are made of sweets on strings
And the moons, the marshmallows eat with
spoons!
I would love it here
But it's not that near!

Georgina Lee (10)
Frieth CEC School, Frieth

The Slime Lake

S ticky slime, make it shine

L ick it and you will kick it

I f you kick it, you will turn sticky

M ake it warm and it will turn slippy

E at slime, you will turn to jelly

L ick your slime, make it so, wait a minute, it is so slow

A t your bath, make a slime bath, it is the same but smaller

K ick your slime, make it bubble, turn around and it will mumble

E ach take a piece and it will bubble.

Emily Forder (8)

Frieth CEC School, Frieth

The Witch!

I can't believe what I saw,
Was a witch riding a dinosaur,
With a hop, with a drop,
With a flippity-flop,
The witch came down,
With a droppity-drop,
The witch came down in a strange place,
And landed on my grandmother's face,
I never knew how much she'd cry,
She dropped down and died!
I still remember my grandmother's face,
And I thought the witch was a disgrace!

Annabelle Groom (10)
Frieth CEC School, Frieth

My Rhyming Bits And Bobs

I had a good time,
Now let's make it rhyme.
I flew through the sky,
On a magpie.

I drove over,
In a Land Rover.
I saw a toad,
He was on the road.

I saw a gnome,
Outside my home.
There was a mime,
Next to the grapevine.

There was a sea,
That was full of tea,
And there were my bits and bobs.

Oscar Deakin (10)
Frieth CEC School, Frieth

Eat Me

Chocolate marshmallows in my face
I didn't know what this place was
But it was ace!
Puffy candy clouds in the sky
Way, way up high
Wow, wow, a burger beach!
I could use that as a feast!
Ice cream raining from the sky
I would never want to say goodbye.

Alice Farrow (8)
Frieth CEC School, Frieth

Higahagajig

In the land of Higahagajig,
Where the billabong boot sings,
The moanie moans to the beat,
Of the mushroom bonger-bing.

Boonies jump like little frogs,
With such bad tempers,
While the fuzz howls like a dog,
With nothing else to centre.

Phoebe Coombs (10)
Frieth CEC School, Frieth

Swimming

I cannot believe how fast I am at swimming
Even though I am winning
The fish are swimming
But they're not winning
I can see them at the beginning

I am almost at the end
It is just around the bend
Then hopefully it will end.

Enzo Xavier Chiappe (10)
Frieth CEC School, Frieth

Pink Fluffy Unicorn On The Moon

There was once a pink fluffy unicorn
dancing on the moon.
She shouted,
"Where is the rainbow in space?"
She got in her spaceship
and looked for the rainbow.
They were behind Earth all along!
She was so happy.

Willow Anderson (9)
Frieth CEC School, Frieth

Pop!

The clouds have legs and feet!
I think they have faces too,
'Cause I heard one bleat!
Sometimes they start and sometimes they stop,
I've seen one skip, I've seen one hop,
But I have never seen one *pop!*

Charlotte Tedder (10)
Frieth CEC School, Frieth

Eco-Friendly Wonderland

If you need to take a break,
And you don't know which path to take,
There's no point going anywhere in this land,
When you can go to the Eco-Friendly Wonderland!
It's amazingly clean,
And the grasshoppers scream,
"It's so green!"
With absolutely no bleach,
Only a very nice beach,
No one ever needs to screech.

George Powlson (10)
King's Lodge Primary School, Chippenham

Crazy Cloud

I reached for a cloud up high,
While I was eating some pie,
And up high I went,
Maybe I had been sent,
To this candyfloss cloud,
Chocolate flavour, it was,
I had my friend over for tea,
At about six thirty-three,
With chips and fish fingers with ketchup,
We played with my ship,
But then we were playing games,
But then we flew before we got the pirates out for the ship,
I was devastated, I was,
After about an hour, we both got bored,
It was a good thing I brought my sword!

Ten minutes later, Isobel was shouting from cloud to cloud,
I was really proud,
I think I'm the first person to have stood on a cloud!

Imogen Hibberd (9)
Old Sarum Primary School, Old Sarum

The Mythical Unicorn Bee

In the sunlight
On a hot summer's day
Flying high like a kite
Something's wanting to play.
Black and yellow with fluttering wings
A unicorn horn and a bottom that stings
Her family's all normal, it's pollen they seek
But it's rainbows she chases, they think she's a freak!
The magic is made when the sun meets the rain
The rainbow is formed, then starts the pain.
Off she flies towards the beautiful sight
But she crashes into something that's fluffy and white.
She thought it was a cloud until she had her crash
Now she turns around and sees the mouthful of grass.
Fluffy and woolly with fur like mine?
No unicorn horn, but hooves that shine...
The woolly shape then says, "Baa!"
Is this why she's come so far?
Then she meets a unicorn bee

She begins to think, *he looks like me!*
Maybe this is where she belongs
In this mythical place where the rainbows are strong.

Lexie Taylor Redman (10)
Old Sarum Primary School, Old Sarum

My Social Media World!

Houses made of iPhone cases,
People on Roblox having races.

Real emojis roaming free,
Faces on Musical.ly bursting with glee!

Holly H was doing the finger dance,
These screens had put people in some sort of trance!

Collins O was faking a girl,
Wearing a necklace with a shiny pink pearl.

Restaurant Tycoon was getting busy,
All the waitresses were getting very dizzy!

Filters were floating in the bright blue sky,
Slowly but surely, they were getting quite high!

"Follow me! Follow me!" everyone screamed,
Videos and photos were covered in memes!

Rebecca Zamolo and Sofie Dossi,
Were doing contortionism on grass which was mossy!

I was on Snapchat in the corner,
Of an iPhone house just on the border!

I got to see Alanna-Kate 34781,
This world has been so much fun!

Isobel Moody (9)
Old Sarum Primary School, Old Sarum

Me And My KitKat Friend

My best friend is a Kit Kat, you know,
I hope that you did hear,
I will tell you such a good story that it will make
you shed a tear,
A tear of joy, my good man,
No need to gloat,
For such a tale would be great without a punchline
and a joke.

Once we'd got up the mountain road,
We had to puff and carry on our load.
We suddenly got up the hill to Roblox World,
Where there was a chill,
It went down my spine,
Would I make it home in time?
Okay, okay, it was going to be fine,
Now I can carry on with my rhyme.

We did the Denis Daily Obby first,
But then KitKat was dying of thirst.
McDonald's Tycoon was very busy,
All the chefs were tired and giddy.

We got home safe, tired and happy,
And that, my friend, was a story so sappy.

Harriet Josephine Langley (9)
Old Sarum Primary School, Old Sarum

The Magical Talking Book

How excited could I be?

I was off with Mum to visit the library!

"Hurry up, Mum, we don't want to be late and miss the bus,

I've been looking forward to this so much, I cannot wait!"

Finally, we got there, but not in time - the doors closed shut.

The talking book was crying her little eyes out.

Mum said, "Never mind, love, maybe another time,

Let's go back home."

In my bedroom, feeling sad,

Magically, the book had crept into my bag.

"Can I stay with you?" she asked.

"Yes, of course you can!" I replied.

What an amazing day I'd had,

I had a friend to read with forever!

Brooke Lewis (9)

Old Sarum Primary School, Old Sarum

Lewandowski

L ove his goals

E ven though he is better than Aubameyang

W ait, he's faster than Ronaldo

A nd a star like him might win him the Golden Boot

N ot in third place, not in second, but first place

D id you know that he also does karate?

O h, he is injured again for the tenth time!

W hat? He's scored again

"S core a good goal!" says a six-year-old

K ind of one of the best goal scorers in history

I like him.

James Tovey (9)
Old Sarum Primary School, Old Sarum

Aliens On Earth

A ll green and slimy,
L istening to rock music,
I rresponsible creatures they are,
E very day, they eat snot burgers,
N ever brush their teeth,
S peak Japanese.

O bviously, they are disgusting,
N aughty cheaters.

E xciting and fun,
A lways weird and clumsy,
R espect others,
T hey play with bananas and apples,
H opefully they'll sleep soon!

Orlagh-Mai Erin Tyrrell (9)
Old Sarum Primary School, Old Sarum

I'm In Candy Land

I look around and the first thing I see
is a swirly-whirly lollipop.

I take a second look around and I see
a whirly river filled with bubblegum soda.

I hear children at the park
that is made out of sugar bark.

I sing a song so bright with glee
which makes me sing so happily.

I had a dream that I could go to Candyland
but I know it's a dream.

I take my last look and then
I disappear...

Elly-Mae Willock (9)
Old Sarum Primary School, Old Sarum

Scented Land

Here at Scented Land,
Smells like cupcakes everywhere.
Letters of your name,
Pencils and rubbers of all kinds.
All you can see is scented stuff.
All prizes are scented.
If you look carefully, it looks a bit like Smiggle.
The sun is made out of a big puffy yellow cushion,
At Scented Land, where everything comes alive.

Lily-Ann Marie Keating (9)
Old Sarum Primary School, Old Sarum

Wonderland

W onderful
O tters on a raft
N ever-ending
D ungeon deep and dark
E scape
R ays of sun
L ight the way
A mazing
N onsensical
D ream.

Owen Otter (9)
Old Sarum Primary School, Old Sarum

Young Writers Information

We hope you have enjoyed reading this book – and that you will continue to in the coming years.

If you're a young writer who enjoys reading and creative writing, or the parent of an enthusiastic poet or story writer, do visit our website **www.youngwriters.co.uk**. Here you will find free competitions, workshops and games, as well as recommended reads, a poetry glossary and our blog. There's lots to keep budding writers motivated to write!

If you would like to order further copies of this book, or any of our other titles, then please give us a call or visit **www.youngwriters.co.uk**.

Young Writers
Remus House
Coltsfoot Drive
Peterborough
PE2 9BF
(01733) 890066
info@youngwriters.co.uk

Join in the conversation!
Tips, news, giveaways and much more!

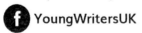 YoungWritersUK 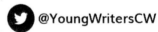 @YoungWritersCW